A Little Paws...
for a time out
with God

uplifting devotions to brighten your day

Inspired
by Faith

A Little Paws...for a time out with God
©Product Concept Mfg., Inc.

A Little Paws...for a time out with God
ISBN 978-1-7325781-1-1

Published by Product Concept Mfg., Inc.
2175 N. Academy Circle #201, Colorado Springs, CO 80909

©2018 Product Concept Mfg., Inc. All rights reserved.

Written and Compiled by Patricia Mitchell
in association with Product Concept Mfg., Inc.

All scripture quotations are from the King James version
of the Bible unless otherwise noted.

Scriptures taken from the Holy Bible,
New International Version®, NIV®.
Copyright © 1973, 1978, 1984 by Biblica, Inc.™
Used by permission of Zondervan.
All rights reserved worldwide.
www.zondervan.com

Sayings not having a credit listed are contributed by writers
for Product Concept Mfg., Inc. or in a rare case,
the author is unknown.

A Little Paws...
for a time out
with God

A cat, I am sure, could walk on a cloud without coming through.

Jules Verne

What greater gift than the love of a cat?
Charles Dickens

She's a cat. She spends her days lazing in the sunshine, and her nights curled contentedly next to (or across the face of) her sleeping human. Food comes with predictable regularity from the hand of same human, along with plenty of cuddles and kisses and lots of tasty treats.

You might not enjoy a pampered pet's leisurely lifestyle, but as God's child, you are as dearly loved – and more! He invites you to wrap yourself in the certainty of His presence, He nourishes you with His spiritual gifts. And He showers you with blessings just to hear you "purr"!

Paws here for cat-connected verses and quotes, uplifting reflections and positive thoughts. May you read with a cat in your lap – and a smile in your heart!

Leave it to a cat to find her own little place in the sun! If there's a ray of light peeking through a gap in the curtains, a cat will take a nap in it. If there's a sunbeam pouring across the floor, a cat will lie down and stretch the length of it. If there's a sun-kissed spot on the patio, a cat will close her eyes and bask in it, savoring each luscious, languid moment.

A Place in the Sun

In your life, God's love is like that ray of light, that warm, sunlit, happy place of rest and repose, pleasure and joy. No matter how dark your skies may seem right now, God waits to flood your heart with the solace of His ever-present love. All you need to do is relax in it. Bask in it. Maybe even take a little catnap in it!

Where can you find His sunshine? In the promises of Scripture to light your way... the inspiration of spiritual songs and verses to put a bounce in your step...the encouraging words of a friend to renew, restore, and refresh your heart. Let the sunshine in! God has a happy place in the sun just for you.

**Dear God, let me find that
happy place of rest and delight
in the sunshine of your love.**

Amen

Keep your face always toward the sunshine –
and shadows will fall behind you.
Walt Whitman

What sunshine is to flowers,
smiles are to humanity. These are but trifles,
to be sure; but scattered along life's pathway,
the good they do is inconceivable.
Joseph Addison

Come unto me...and I will give you rest.
Matthew 11:28

A flower cannot blossom without sunshine,
and man cannot live without love.
Friedrich Max Müller

There is no duty we so underrate
as the duty of being happy.
Robert Louis Stevenson

Far away there in the sunshine are my
highest aspirations. I may not reach them,
but I can look up and see their beauty,
believe in them, and try to follow where they lead.
Louisa May Alcott

A good laugh is sunshine in the house.
William Makepeace Thackeray

Whoever possesses God is happy.
Augustine

When a cat's hungry, you know it! He doesn't ask once and then patiently wait until you're ready to serve. No. He'll howl and yowl and meow until you produce a plate of food and set it down in front of him. Persistence (and a lot of noise) gets results every time!

Hungry?

When you take your wants and needs to God, do you ask once, and then expect results to suddenly appear...dropping down from the sky, perhaps? It rarely happens that way. More often than not, God encourages you to ask again and again...and again. Even for what seems like a long time. You see, perseverance in prayer tests the strength and permanence of your desire. It opens you to His wisdom as you seek His will, think and rethink, visit and revisit, your request. And sometimes, your perseverance, translated into practical action, is exactly what God uses to bring you what you've been praying for all along!

What are you hungry for? Ask God. Unless it drops down from the sky (praying for rain?) ask again. Make some noise! Persevere in prayer!

**Dear God, keep me persistent in prayer,
asking according to Your will.**
Amen

The simple heart that freely asks in love, obtains.
John Greenleaf Whittier

Persistent people begin their success
where others end in failure.
Edward Eggleston

Pray without ceasing.
1 Thessalonians 5:17

Prayer is not eloquence,
but earnestness.
Hannah More

If you wish success in life,
make perseverance your bosom friend.
Joseph Addison

Meow-y Thanks

I have a loud meow-er
I'm not afraid to use!
I'll meow for treats and nibbles—
Anything I choose!
But then my loving human
Must of course agree,
So this meow means "thank you"
For how you care for me!"

Planning to log on? There's a cat taking a nap on the keyboard. Fine. That can wait. So you'll dive into the novel you've been itching to read...but a cat's curled up in your comfiest chair. Okay. How about making some progress on the jigsaw puzzle that...uh-oh... someone forgot to lay the cat-proof cover over it last night. Sigh!

Our Plans and Other Plans

You've made some well-thought-out plans for the near future. But there are times, in life-changing ways, God turns those plans upside down. It's never His intention to thwart your hopes and dreams, or to cause you pain, but to guide you in the direction He would have you go. After all, your good plans might sidestep the challenge God will use to enhance and strengthen your character, courage, and ingenuity. Your plans might fail to foresee the change in circumstances that will bring unimagined experiences and opportunities into your life.

If your plans have fallen apart like a cat-scattered jigsaw puzzle, scoop up the pieces and start putting them together. You might be surprised at the splendid new picture God has in mind for you!

Dear God, You alone know what the future will bring. Open my eyes to Your plans for my life.
Amen

The Cat's Nap

Straight across the pages
Of an open book,
Hiding in the crevice
Of a secret nook—
Middle of the sofa,
Perched atop the fridge,
Underneath the table,
Balanced on a ledge—
Corner of a cupboard,
Armrest of a chair—
Where is kitty sleeping?
Could be anywhere!

Change, indeed, is painful, yet ever needful.
Thomas Carlyle

"For I know the plans I have for you,"
declares the Lord, "plans to prosper you
and not to harm you,
plans to give you hope and a future."
Jeremiah 29:11 NIV

Why do we shrink from change?
What can come into being save by change?
Marcus Aurelius

Cease to inquire what the future has in store,
and take as a gift whatever the day brings forth.
Horace

Rejoice in the things that are present;
all else is beyond thee.
Michel de Montaigne

If you have ever visited an animal shelter or attended an adoption event, you knew when you had found your purrfect forever friend. Maybe it was the variegated stripes, the perky ringed tail, the whimsical spots, or the tuxedo tie that caught your attention – but what captured your heart was the stroke of a fuzzy face in the palm of your hand that said in every way, "I completely trust you."

A Matter of Trust

Have you ever given your complete trust to God? Just as you would promise to love, protect, nourish, and delight in your furry friend, so God promises to love, protect, nourish, and delight in you. You can trust Him to know your needs. You can trust Him to feed you with the right spiritual food. You can trust Him to provide for you now and forever.

Perhaps you're afraid to trust because you have been let down in the past. Yes, human relationships can fail and life circumstances can change. Only God, the unchangeable, can provide the security you need and crave. Put yourself in His arms. With complete confidence, place all your trust in Him.

**Dear God, help me learn to put
my trust in You,
and not rely on my own understanding.
Amen**

Blessed are all they that put their trust in him.
Psalm 2:12

All I have seen teaches me to trust
the Creator for all I have not seen.
Ralph Waldo Emerson

Trust the past to God's mercy,
the present to God's love,
and the future to God's providence.
Augustine

Pray, and let God worry.
Martin Luther

Trust wholly in Christ.
John Wycliffe

I am trusting Thee, Lord Jesus;
Never let me fall—
I am trusting Thee forever,
And for all!

Frances R. Havergal

When we walk with the Lord
in the light of His Word,
What a glory He sheds on our way!
While we do His good will,
He abides with us still,
And with all who will trust and obey.

John H. Sammis

When peace, like a river, attendeth my way,
When sorrows like sea billows roll;
Whatever my lot Thou hast taught me to say,
"It is well, it is well, with my soul."

Horatio Spafford

When one cat enters the family, she's often followed by another. Then another. And sometimes another...or several "anothers"! But no matter how many kitties share home and heart, each one has a different, unique personality.

You've Got Purrsonality!

Your personality is uniquely yours. You have been placed in a particular family and possess innate gifts. You have lived through a range of experiences, made and continue to make certain decisions and respond in a particular way to the world around you. That's why, when you see others through God's eyes, you see nothing less than a bright, marvelous, and awe-inspiring kaleidoscope of living, thinking, active, unique people. And you're one of them!

Don't forget to celebrate what's unique about you – the things about you that bring joy to your heart and to the hearts of others. The ways you show kindness, gentleness, thoughtfulness. Your ability to listen. The things you do and say to show you care. These are just a few of the blessings of your purrfect purrsonality!

**Dear God, allow me to look at myself
and others through Your eyes of love!**
Amen

Purrsonalities

Classy, sassy,
Walks with pride—
Anxious, edgy,
Likes to hide.
Shabby, scruffy,
Stately, neat—
Frisky, feisty,
Fast on feet.
Curious, clever,
Always keen—

Watchful, wary,
Rarely seen.
Bratty, chatty,
Breaks the rules –
Peaceful, tranquil,
Calm and cool.
Cuddly, snuggly,
High demand –
Splendid, awesome –
All are grand!

A cat's keen hearing can detect the slightest of sounds. Though seemingly sound asleep, his ears perk up at a practically imperceptible click or chirp, instantly swiveling toward the noise. But if we shout his name and he's not ready to come? Not a twitch. Not a notice. Not a peek in your direction.

Impromptu Invitation

Temptation whispers. We're all ears! But when God calls...Although we know we should listen, we don't always want to. Like a kitten chasing a sunbeam, we're just too busy to stop what we're doing at the moment. Later, we might remember the quiet pull, the gentle nudge, the compelling thought – but what was it? More often than not, poof! It's gone.

God's voice can come when you least expect it. Though He doesn't command you to drop everything and stand at attention, He invites your thoughts to turn to Him for a few moments. Be receptive to his message. Perhaps He has an idea or an insight for you. A word of caution or encouragement. Or just the heartwarming reassurance of His love.

Dear God, when You speak, turn my heart and mind to the sound of Your voice.
Amen

We gain the strength
of the temptation we resist.
Ralph Waldo Emerson

We usually know what we can do,
but temptation shows us who we are.
Thomas à Kempis

The wisdom that is from above is first pure,
then peaceable, gentle, and easy to be entreated,
full of mercy and good fruits,
without partiality, and without hypocrisy.
James 3:17

Speak, LORD; for thy servant heareth.
1 Samuel 3:9

We hear voices in solitude,
we never hear in the hurry and turmoil of life;
we receive counsels and comforts we get
under no other condition.

Amelia Barr

The great blessings of mankind are within us,
and within our reach; but we shut our eyes,
and like people in the dark, fall short of the very
thing we search for without finding it.

Seneca

A wise man will hear,
and will increase learning;
and a man of understanding shall attain
unto wise counsels.

Proverbs 1:5

Kittens at play – it's impossible to watch without smiling! There's something about their carefree abandon that seems remote to us. But as the years pass, we tend to relegate recreation to "when we have time," which, in our busy lives, translates to, "rarely, if ever"!

For the Fun of It

Play is a God-given way to rest, relax, and recharge. Whether it's a game of solitaire or team sport, an afternoon doodling or meeting up with friends, play is just as necessary to you as it is for kids and kittens alike. It gives you a chance to step away from your worries and problems, and do something that lets your true self breathe and stretch. What's more, you'll return to your daily responsibilities with a clearer mind, often finding that those worries and problems weren't as big as they had looked to you earlier!

How would you like to play today? Give it a try – and if your fun includes a lively feline, so much the better!

**Dear God, let me rediscover
the gift of play...
grant me the blessing of
laughter and joy.
Amen**

It's great to be great,
but it's greater to be human.
Will Rogers

The fruit of the Spirit is love, joy...
Galatians 5:22

When I play with my cat,
who knows if I am not a pastime
to her more than she is to me?
Michel de Montaigne

Nothing like a little judicious levity.
Robert Louis Stevenson

Stretch out your hand and take
the world's wide gift of Joy and Beauty.
Corinne Roosevelt Robinson

You can discover more about
a person in an hour of play than
in a year of conversation.
Plato

To finish the moment,
to find the journey's end in
every step of the road,
to live the greatest number of good hours,
is wisdom.
Ralph Waldo Emerson

The true object of all human life is play.
G. K. Chesterton

It's 2 a.m.! But the cat doesn't care about the clock. She's thinking about a treat, or breakfast, or petting, or playing, so she slips beside her human's ear and begins to wail. If her human remains abed, she might take several strolls across the pillows, or start batting around whatever she can find – perhaps said human's cell phone.

Meow in the Night

Being awakened by meows and yowls in the middle of the night might leave any one of us feeling a little grumpy in the morning. Yet when our own wants and worries, problems and concerns keep us tossing and turning into the wee hours of the morning, we're invited to call out – wail, if we want! – to God. He keeps no "do not disturb" hours, and grumpy just isn't who He is – ever. Know that He remains awake, awaiting the prayers and petitions that come to Him at any time, day or night.

The next time a little feline starts to prowl and yowl in the nighttime hours, remember how welcome you are to talk to God – any time you want to.

**Dear God, thank You,
for I can call whenever I need to.
You are always attentive to my cry!
Amen**

There are moments when,
whatever be the attitude of the body,
the soul is on its knees.
Victor Hugo

The sovereign cure for worry is prayer.
William James

If you only knock long enough
and loud enough at the gate,
you are sure to wake up somebody.
Henry Wadsworth Longfellow

In the day of my trouble
I will call upon thee:
for thou wilt answer me.
Psalm 86:7

Pussy-cat, Pussy-cat

Pussy-cat, pussy-cat,
where have you been?
I've been to London
to visit the Queen.
Pussy-cat, pussy-cat,
what did you there?
I frightened a little mouse
under her chair!
"MEOWW!"

Traditional Nursery Rhyme

Some adopted kitties adjust quickly to a new home, and immediately explore every corner of their domain. Others, however, instantly hide – under the bed, in a closet, behind a couch. So you lure them out with cajoling words and savory tidbits, assuring the timid little hearts that they're in a good place, a warm, loving, and welcoming place.

Out of Hiding

Sometimes we're in hiding from God. Hiding, perhaps, because we feel uncomfortable about something we've said or done. Hiding, because we're not sure how to speak to God, given our jumbled thoughts. Hiding, because it just doesn't seem logical that God's forgiveness could apply to us.

But God wants to forgive, whatever the error! He is the source of clarity and confidence. So He reaches out to you through the words of Scripture, reminding you that He understands and earnestly desires to renew and restore your relationship to Him. He lures you out of hiding with the guarantee of His love, the assurance of His forgiveness, and the promise of His peace. With Him, you're always in a safe place!

**Dear God, no matter what I have done,
let me never doubt Your
willingness to forgive!**
Amen

Come, and let us return unto the LORD.
Hosea 6:1

It's only those who do nothing that make
no mistakes, I suppose.
Joseph Conrad

Whatever with the past is gone;
the best is always yet to come.
Lucy Larcom

When you go to bed at night,
have for your pillow three things –
love, hope, and forgiveness.
And you will awaken in the morning
with a song in your heart.
Victor Hugo

Create in me a clean heart,
O God;
and renew a right spirit within me.
Psalm 51:10

I have been all things unholy;
if God can work through me,
He can work through anyone.
Francis of Assisi

As far as the east is from the west,
so far hath he removed our
transgressions from us.
Psalm 103:12

Let the past drift away with the water.
Proverb

You get to know your feline friends – and your human ones, too – by regularly interacting with them. Only through interaction can you discover their likes and dislikes, and discern their habits and temperament. At the same time, they are getting to know you. Without interaction, the bond between you has little chance of forming, much less strengthening.

Interactive Living

As important as building and strengthening bonds between you and your two-legged and four-legged friends, even more important is building and strengthening your relationship with God. It happens when you interact with Him in prayer (you speak, He listens)...through the words of Scripture (He speaks, you listen)...by desiring the gifts of His Spirit (you ask, He gives, you receive). Just as in any other relationship, your knowledge of Him increases the more you learn of Him, and your love for Him increases the more you realize how much He loves and cares for you.

The bond between you and your God is a living, giving, and growing relationship. And all relationships thrive on interaction, one with another. Live interactively with Him!

**Dear God, let our relationship thrive
as I turn my heart and mind to You!**
Amen

There is no hope or joy except in human relations.
Antoine de Saint-Exupery

All the wealth of the world
cannot be compared with the happiness
of living together happily united.
Marie-Marguerite d'Youville

There is no wilderness like a life
without friends; friendship multiplies blessings
and minimizes misfortunes; it is a unique remedy
against adversity, and it soothes the soul.
Baltasar Gracian

I have called you friends;
for all things that I have heard of my Father
I have made known unto you.
John 15:15

We take care of our health,
we lay up money, we make our roof tight
and our clothing sufficient,
but who provides wisely that he shall not
be wanting in the best property of all—friends?
Ralph Waldo Emerson

My only sketch, profile,
of heaven is a large blue sky, and larger
than the biggest I have seen in June,
and in it are my friends—every one of them.
Emily Dickinson

Good friendships are fragile things and require as
much care as any other fragile and precious thing.
Randolph Bourne

Friendship is a plant that must often be watered.
Proverb

Actions, not words, are the true criterion
of the attachment of friends.
George Washington

"Dear little one, I think you know my routine better than I do myself! You're at the foot of my bed in the morning, and you scamper ahead of me as I go into the kitchen. You're at the door when I come home in the evening, and you place yourself right where your food bowl appears. But if tonight I don't have time to sit on the sofa and make a lap for you while I read, will you forgive me? Tomorrow, I promise you!"

Rut or Routine?

A daily routine allows us to use time wisely and well. It enables us to make present and future plans and commitments with some amount of certainty, and set reasonable, doable goals for ourselves. Sometimes, however, a routine morphs into a rut.

You've fallen into a rut when you're doing what you're supposed to do, but with little joy or satisfaction. Despite your activity, you're unable to make, or see, progress. While your kitty might be quite pleased with your predictability, you are not. You need a change! Perhaps not a complete overhaul of how you spend your time, but something to get you out of the rut. It can be as easy – and as pleasant – as taking a little time to pamper yourself, or doing what you keep putting off until "later." Surprise yourself with something different!

**Dear God, open my imagination to what
I can do with my time today!**
Amen

We always have time enough, if we will use it aright.
Johann Wolfgang von Goethe

By going over your day in imagination
before you begin it, you can begin
acting successfully at any moment.
Dorothea Brande

Dost thou love life?
Then do not squander time,
for that's the stuff life is made of.
Benjamin Franklin

Be renewed in the spirit of your mind.
Ephesians 4:23

May you live all the days of your life.
Jonathan Swift

A day's impact is better than
a month of dead pull.
Oliver Wendell Holmes Jr.

He who every morning plans the
transactions of the day and follows out
that plan carries a thread that will guide him
through the labyrinth of the most busy life....
If the disposal of time is surrendered merely
to the chance of incident, chaos will soon reign.
Victor Hugo

Write it on your heart that every day
is the best day in the year.
Ralph Waldo Emerson

"Where did you come from, little kitty? Where do you belong? You sauntered up to my door and meowed the entrance open. And then, without further ado, you strolled into the kitchen, looked at the cupboard, looked at the counter, and looked at me. Okay, I get it. Yet I can only wonder what sign or signal pointed you in my direction!"

Come Back!

Sometimes even the most comfortable house-cat decides to venture away from home. Maybe she's compelled to wander by the very thing that prompts us to roam away from God – curiosity. We're curious what it would be like to do what it seems everyone else is doing. Our reason tells us there's little harm in trying, so we explore attitudes and activities that go against God's will for us. And like the curious cat, we sometimes get lost.

If you don't feel as comfortably at home with God as you'd like to, stop wandering around looking for Him. There's no need – He knows where you are. Allow Him to come to you, pick you up, brush you off, and carry you back to where you belong.

**No matter where I've strayed, dear God,
You will bring me back to You!
Amen**

Come In!

Pretty kitty,
I've seen your eyes
that catch the glint
of the summer sun
peeking through the hedge—
and then, another day,
a streak of gray from
hiding place to hiding place
in the garden's overgrown shrubs...
Pretty kitty,
inching shyly toward my kitchen door,

a pleading look,
a cautious stand—
ready, at any moment to bound away
if you needed to.
Pretty kitty,
look at you!
Where you've come from,
I don't know,
but, pretty kitty,
please come in.
Don't be afraid...
you've found a home with me.

The home of a cat bears telltale signs of her presence. A patch of the sofa's upholstery "polished" to a sheen...paint rubbed away near the bottom of a door jamb... wicker twigs loosened on the back of a chair where two pairs of claws have done their work. She's establishing her scent. She's marking her space. It's her way of making a house a home.

Marked by Love

Through the gift of faith, God's Spirit claims you as His own. His continued work in your heart and mind marks the values you live by, the objectives you go after, the choices you make, and your everyday words, actions, and relationships. When living, active faith engages you, there's little room for negative influences and destructive thoughts to gain a foothold. You are occupied by God, established in His love. You are His territory.

Ever have a cat nudge and rub you with her chin? She's saying that she loves you, and, what's more, you belong to her. God "nudges" you for the same reason. He loves you, and you belong to Him.

**Dear God, thank You for marking me
as Your own with the gift
of faith in Jesus!
Amen**

To live without loving is
not really to live.
Molière

Our perfection certainly consists
in knowing God and ourselves.
Angela of Foligno

Love cannot endure indifference.
It needs to be wanted.
Henry Ward Beecher

It is only by forgetting yourself
that you draw nearer to God.
Henry David Thoreau

If you would be loved,
love and be lovable.
Benjamin Franklin

Let us remember that within us,
there is a palace of
immense magnificence.
Teresa of Ávila

Love is space and time
measured by the heart.
Marcel Proust

We know what we are,
but know not what we may be.
William Shakespeare

"Aww, poor kitty! You seem to sense that it's time to see your doctor. Your eyes are as wide as saucers, your ears at attention for any move I might make toward your carrier. You're ready to dart under the dresser, aren't you? So I'll come cooing and smiling like I always do, with a treat in my hand...too late! You're crouched tight where you know I can't reach! Aww, poor me!"

Good Grief

It's deeply personal. One difficult diagnosis, one unfortunate event, one piece of bad news can put our thoughts, plans, and even relationships on trial. Is this really God's plan?

In a way, perhaps it is. He permits adversity to happen, and through it, He often works amazing things. Yes, there's grief, and you have every need to grieve. But hold tight to God while you grieve, and let Him hold tight to you. Allow His comfort to console you, His strength to support you, and His promises to fill your heart with hope. Rest your fears as He lights your way ahead of you, step by step. In time, you may look back and, even with a tear in your eye, see that there was good in the grief. It was good grief.

Dear God, when adversity comes my way, help me handle it with You, in Your way.
Amen

Praise be to...the God of all comfort,
who comforts us in all our troubles,
so that we can comfort those in any trouble with
the comfort we ourselves receive from God.
2 Corinthians 1:3-4 NIV

Affliction comes to us all not to make us sad,
but sober; not to make us sorry, but wise;
not to make us despondent,
but by the darkness to refresh us.
Henry Ward Beecher

All shall be well, and all shall be well,
and all manner of things shall be well.
Julian of Norwich

Acceptance of what has happened
is the first step to overcoming the
consequences of any misfortune.
William James

Hope is the thing with feathers
That perches in the soul,
And sings the tune without the words,
And never stops at all.

Emily Dickinson

Let nothing disturb you,
Let nothing frighten you,
All things are passing away:
God never changes,
Patience obtains all things.
Whoever has God lacks nothing;
God alone suffices.

Teresa of Avila

Admit it – our cats are thoroughly spoiled! By us. Even when the sparkly, tingly toys are chased once across the room and never touched again, or the organic gourmet treats are summarily ignored, we don't stop buying them. After all, you never know – hey, maybe this long, lavish, fluffy (and pricey) feather will tickle her feline fancy!

Spoiler Alert

There's joy in finding just the right gift for someone – including those four-legged some-ones who live with us. If the latest doodad seems unappreciated, we might throw our hands up in dismay, but not without a smile.

Every day, God sends us blessings – those "toys and treats" that He showers down on us. Sometimes we appreciate them – a startling sunrise, a fragrant garden, a friendly smile, a delightful song – but sometimes they're barely noticed. We rush right past them – those small, ordinary joys that are there every day – search-ing instead for a big, showy extravaganza that we think we need for happiness.

Today, look around. Expect to find something to smile about. Let God spoil you with blessings!

Dear God, open my eyes to the wonders that are all around me, and grant me true appreciation for all the ways you bless me!
Amen

When I first open my eyes upon the
morning meadows and look out upon the
beautiful world, I thank God I am alive.
Ralph Waldo Emerson

Sunshine is delicious, rain is refreshing,
wind braces us up, snow is exhilarating;
there is really no such thing as bad weather,
only different kinds of good weather.
John Ruskin

All the great blessings of my life are
present in my thoughts today.
Phoebe Cary

Let the thankful heart sweep through
the day and, as the magnet finds the iron,
so it will find, in every hour,
some heavenly blessings!
Henry Ward Beecher

All the Best

Toys and treats
Home and hearth
Hide and seek
Hugs and heart
What more can I do?

Balls and bells,
Purrs and trills,
Pranks and spells
Jumps and spills—
Joy with each mew!

Snooze and stretch,
Yawn and wake,
Sit and watch,
Eat and play —
All the best for you!

"My motor is running full throttle! Life is good. I've got a full belly, a soft pillow, and a ray of sunshine, and I'm the best-blessed cat in the world. Why dwell on the past? It's past! Why fear the future? It's not here! Right now, I'm good, and I'm not afraid to purr about it!"

Purr Like You Mean It!

Plenty of people make it their business to point out what's wrong with the world. How about what's right with the world?

When you see things that are going right, tell yourself. Tell others. When you do, something startling happens – you begin to notice a whole lot of other things that are going amazingly right, as well as many other situations and events that aren't as calamitous as you had imagined. When you talk about what's going right with you, others are prompted to talk about what's going right with them. Now your awareness of all the good things out there has expanded even further!

There are enough naysayers around. When you're happy, purr like you know it. Purr like you mean it!

Dear God, open my eyes to good and positive things, and to all that is going well in my life.
Amen

What we see depends mainly
on what we look for.
John Lubbock

O give thanks unto the LORD;
for he is good: because his mercy
endureth for ever.
Psalm 118:1

The greater part of our happiness
or misery depends on our dispositions,
and not upon our circumstances.
Martha Washington

Events, circumstances, etc.,
have their origin in ourselves.
They spring from seeds which
we have sown.
Henry David Thoreau

Could we change our attitude,
we should not only see life differently,
but life itself would come to be different.
Life would undergo a change of appearance
because we ourselves had undergone
a change in attitude.

Katherine Mansfield

The world is a looking-glass and gives back
to every man the reflection of his own face.
Frown at it, and it will in turn look sourly upon you;
laugh at it and with it,
and it is a jolly, kind companion.

William Makepeace Thackeray

Dream lofty dreams, and as you dream,
so shall you become.
Your vision is the promise of what
you shall at last unveil.

John Ruskin

"You look up at me and lick your paw so innocently! But I see the flower pot's been tipped over (again!) and clumps of soil are spread across the floor. How did that happen? You were tempted by a dangling leaf, perhaps. Or a little fun digging in the dirt was too much to resist. Naughty, naughty kitty!"

Real Love

Many a flowerpot, bowl, knickknack, and vase have succumbed to the paws of a cat! Yet the naughty girl still has our love. Even as we're sweeping up the shards, we're more concerned with the possibility of a splinter lodged in her paw than we are with the loss of an ornament.

Our continuing love for a naughty kitty is one way to understand the mystery of God's continuing love for us, no matter what we do! Despite our many actions that displease Him, He's more concerned with how we may have hurt ourselves. That's real love!

If there are broken pieces in your life, let Him sweep them up. Allow His forgiveness to remove the splinters that continue to hurt you, and let the balm of His love heal the wound inside your heart.

**Dear God, You know what has happened.
Let me come to You,
assured of Your everlasting love.
Amen**

One word frees us of all the weight
and pain of life: That word is love.
Sophocles

The LORD hath appeared of old unto me,
saying, Yea, I have loved thee
with an everlasting love:
therefore with lovingkindness
have I drawn thee.
Jeremiah 31:3

Love rules without rules.
Proverb

Love is the nature of God,
He can do no other.
Angelus Silesius

God is love.
1 John 4:8

Love Is

True love is kind, and gentle,
even where there's wrong...
It's wise and understanding,
humble, firm, and strong.
True love speaks words of healing,
Actions cause no pain...
It means that there's forgiveness,
Even yet again.
True love cares more for others,
Putting self aside.
Of all that comes and passes,
Love will still abide.

Adapted from 1 Corinthians 13

Her eyes wide, her gaze intent...expressive...expectant. I stopped. Her calico face pressed against the door of her enclosure. But when I continued down the row, she silently retreated to the farthest corner. Then I returned, and she sprang to life again, meeting me at the door. What else could I do? I hooked the sign in my hand to the latch: ADOPTED.

Life Changes

You change a life when you adopt a cat. She moves from shelter to home...from being one among many to one uniquely yours.

In a similar way, God changes our lives when He adopts us as His daughters and sons. We're no longer seeking shelter and security in the transient power of money, status, or human strategies. Instead, we have a home – a strong, permanent foundation – in His presence and His promises. We're not our old selves anymore. Through the gifts of His Spirit, He restores and renews us, making us uniquely His.

Today, let your heart and mind relax in the home you have with Him. Savor His peace and the certainty of His care. Relish the love. Embrace the lasting joy.

Thank You, dear God, for the place
You have brought me to!
Amen

Ye have received the Spirit of adoption,
whereby we cry, Abba, Father.
Romans 8:15

The Spiritual Life is the gift of the
Living Spirit. The spiritual man is no
mere development of the Natural man.
He is a New Creation born from Above.
Henry Drummond

Faith is to believe what you do not see;
the reward of this faith is to see
what you believe.
Augustine

The best thing must be to flee
from all to the All.
Teresa of Avila

Faith is an excitement and an enthusiasm:
it is a condition of intellectual magnificence to
which we must cling as to a treasure,
and not squander on our way through life
in the small coin of empty words.
George Sand

If any man be in Christ, he is a new creature:
old things are passed away; behold,
all things are become new.
2 Corinthians 5:17

The majority of men live without being
thoroughly conscious that they
are spiritual beings.
Søren Kierkegaard

Cats must have built-in self-esteem! They'll strut through the house as if they make the mortgage payment, and they'll defend their space on the patio against all comers (including the two-legged person who laid the patio pavers). Cats have an important place in the world – and they know it!

The Cat's Meow

Leonardo da Vinci is credited with noting that "the smallest feline is a masterpiece." Cat-lovers believe it – and so do their cats! No matter where they are or what they look like, cats do not doubt themselves or their place in the world.

Unlike our feline friends, many among us struggle with a positive self-image. It's not easy to forget harsh criticism or distressing memories. Yet there's one overriding and eternal fact: you're God's creation.

You have life because God breathed it into you. You possess a place in the world because God put you here. You have been given the gifts of presence and purpose because God has a plan for you. Whenever you're running low on self-esteem, remember: you're a God-made masterpiece. You're the cat's meow!

**Dear God, flood my heart and mind
with the realization that I am fearfully
and wonderfully made.**
Amen

How can we send the highest love
to another if we do not
have it for ourselves?
Prentice Mulford

That kind of life is most happy
which affords us most opportunities
of gaining our own esteem.
Samuel Johnson

He who undervalues himself is
justly undervalued by others.
William Hazlitt

I care not so much what I am to
others as what I am to myself.
I will be rich by myself, and not by borrowing.
Michel de Montaigne

If you want to be respected by others,
the great thing is to respect yourself.
Only by that, only by self-respect
will you compel others to respect you.
Fyodor Dostoyevsky

A man cannot be comfortable
without his own approval.
Mark Twain

Above all things, revere yourself.
Pythagoras

In quietness and in confidence
shall be your strength.
Isaiah 30:15

"Pretty kitty, I agree, this was a cozy, comfy, and snuggly sit an hour ago, but now my legs are cramped and I need to stand up. I shift, but you merely open one eye a slit that says, 'Don't move! I'm just fine, and you're disturbing me.' Sigh! Pretty kitty, may I shift around? Just a teensy, weensy bit?"

Do Move!

Cats don't like to get up before they're ready to get up. An alarm clock is nothing more than a signal best ignored, and certainly not a reason to leave the warm comfort of bed. For the humans who share same bed, however, it's an entirely different matter. In many ways, we don't like to be moved, either. After we've found our comfort zone, we're loathe to leave it. Our habitual ways of doing things, of thinking, of viewing the world generally stay nicely nestled down in their niche...until we're forcibly moved. Something nudges, pushes, shoves us away from where we think we've been quite cozy!

Ready or not, you might be prodded to move out of your comfort zone. When it happens, don't go back to sleep. Do move to greater heights and wider boundaries!

Dear God, give me the courage to explore beyond the comfort of what's familiar to me.
Amen

Don't Move!

Don't bother me!
Just let me sleep
And keep my dreams
Intact!
I'm fine, you know,
I see no glow
In going out,
In fact.
When I arise,
I'll blink my eyes
And, being wise,
React

To what looks good –
Yes, treats and food
Attract.
So let me be,
I'm fine, you see,
For I'm a cat,
And that's
That.

It's been claimed that "dogs have masters, cats have staff." Although cats may be more independent than dogs, they still need more than someone simply handing out food and water. A cat thrives when her human companion is present – ideally, with a ready lap and open arms.

Being There

When we think about doing things for others, we think "things" – say, baking a tray of cookies, assisting with a difficult chore, or driving a friend to an appointment. While all those activities are helpful, there's something else equally, and sometimes more, necessary – simply being there. Being willing to listen. To pay attention. To empathize and to care.

Your presence can mean more than any words can say. Just knowing that someone cares can lighten the load, lift the spirit, and comfort a saddened heart. Sure, listening may not seem like much, but put yourself in their place. Imagine the quiet comfort of knowing someone is concerned enough to hear what they have to say without interrupting. You may or may not be able to help in other ways, but your time, attention, and listening ear can make all the difference.

Dear God, let me be the one who truly listens to others, as You listen to me.
Amen

A good listener is not only popular everywhere,
but after a while,
he knows something.
Wilson Mizner

The greatest compliment that was ever
paid me was when one asked me what I thought,
and attended to my answer.
Henry David Thoreau

To listen well is as powerful a means
of influence as to talk well,
and is as essential to all true conversation.
Proverb

Wisdom is the reward you get
for a lifetime of listening when you
would have rather talked.
Mark Twain

Listening well and answering well
is one of the greatest perfections that can
be obtained in conversation.
François de La Rochefoucauld

Encourage one another and
build each other up,
just as in fact you are doing.
1 Thessalonians 5:11 NIV

We have two ears and one mouth
so that we can listen twice as
much as we speak.
Epictetus

We convince by our presence.
Walt Whitman

*One, then another, then
another...until it's many,
many too many cats. Her heart
was big, her intentions were
generous, her love was abundant,
but her home was small. She
yearned to take care of them
all, but couldn't do it. No one
could. The burden was just too
great for one to bear alone.*

You Can Do It

Occasionally there's a headline-grabbing cat-hoarder story. How a good intention turned into a sad situation for both human and cats is something we certainly can understand. We have all had times when we have bitten off more than we can chew!

While our imaginations may lead us to believe that we can accomplish anything we're truly passionate about, the fact is, we can't. We have our limitations. It might be ability, or resources, or opportunity. But what a comfort to consider that God is limited by none of those things! He is all-powerful.

He possesses the world and everything in it. God has put in your path many feasible and doable opportunities to love Him and to love others. You have the ability. Consider what you can do today!

Thank You, God, for the abundance of love
You shower on me!
Amen

A pint can't hold a quart –
if it holds a pint
it is doing all that can be expected of it.
Margaret Deland

Happy the man who early learns the
wide chasm that lies between
his wishes and his powers.
Johann Wolfgang von Goethe

Which of you, intending to build a tower,
sitteth not down first, and counteth the cost,
whether he have sufficient to finish it?
Luke 14:28

What had seemed easy in imagination
was rather hard in reality.
Lucy Maud Montgomery

With God nothing shall be impossible.
Luke 1:37

Cats All Around

Cats on the porch and cats in the garden,
Cats all over the house!
It's certain this place will never be entered
By dogs, or rats, or a mouse!

Cats energetic, cats calm and sweet,
Cats reserved and aloof—
Oh look! There's a ring-tailed tom and a tabby
Sitting up on the roof!

Cats of all stripes and patches and colors,
Cats and kittens galore!
Cats to remember, cats to come home to!
(In heaven, I hope there are more!)

"So which of us is your favorite?" Three sweet faces peer up expectantly as if to ask the question. Favorite? "Silly kitties, your presence, your quirks and crazy antics, make this family what it is – us together! There are no favorites here – only deep-down love for each of you!"

Playing Favorites

As children, many of us wondered who among our siblings was Mommy's or Daddy's favorite. Not until later in life did we realize how parents can deeply love each child, as different as kids may be in ability, interests, and personality!

God's love for you goes even deeper. No matter how much experience and insight you may possess, you will not be able to comprehend the depth and breadth of God's love for you. His love remains unchanged regardless of who or where you are, your failures or achievements, your struggles or talents. So God has made it easy on you – He doesn't ask you to understand how it's possible He can love every person in the world. All He asks is for you to accept the love He has for you!

**Dear God, although I don't understand
Your love, thank You for the great love
You have for me!
Amen**

Keep me as the apple of the eye,
hide me under the shadow of thy wings.
Psalm 17:8

Why should God need us,
unless it were to give us His love?
Henri Bergson

God loves each of us as if there
were only one of us.
Augustine

If man was not made for God,
why is he only happy in God?
If man was made for God,
why is he so opposed to God?
Blaise Pascal

God enters by a private door into every individual.
Ralph Waldo Emerson

That ye, being rooted and grounded in love,
May be able to comprehend with all saints what is
the breadth, and length, and depth, and height;
And to know the love of Christ, which passeth
knowledge, that ye might be filled with
all the fulness of God.

Ephesians 3:17-19

But God, who is the beginning of all things,
is not to be regarded as a composite being, lest
perchance there should be found to exist elements
prior to the beginning itself, out of which everything
is composed, whatever that be which
is called composite.

Origen

God's delight is in the communication
of Himself, His own happiness to everyone
according to his or her capacity. He does everything
that is good, righteous, and lovely for its own sake,
because it is good, righteous and lovely.

William Law

*"Ah, discovered at last!
Huddled in a corner of the
closet, a tight, compact little
muffin. Your wary, worried eyes
betray your pain. You don't know
I can help you...but you realize
that something's not right,
and you want to hide your
vulnerability."*

Healing Hands

When a cat is sick, she puts on a brave face. After all, in nature, visible weakness can tempt a predator. A beloved housecat does not know that her human companion will not harm her, but take her to where there are medicines and healing hands. We often attempt to hide our most private sorrows and pains, because we – not unlike our sick kitty – realize that our weakness may make us vulnerable to the scorn or criticism of others. We don't run to God with our problems because we're convinced we must handle them ourselves, or simply live with them. We fail to truly realize that God can, and does, heal our wounds.

There's nothing to hide. God already knows your every weakness, every sorrow. Why not put yourself into His healing hands?

Dear God, please heal the wounds of my heart so that I may find joy in life again.
Amen

We know what we are now,
but not what we may become.
William Shakespeare

Health and cheerfulness mutually
beget each other.
Joseph Addison

Have mercy upon me, O LORD;
for I am weak: O LORD, heal me;
for my bones are vexed.
Psalm 6:2

There is no despair so absolute as
that which comes with the first moments
of our first great sorrow,
when we have not yet known what
it is to have suffered and to be healed,
to have despaired and have recovered hope.
George Eliot

Heal me, O LORD, and I shall be healed;
save me, and I shall be saved.
Jeremiah 17:14

Always laugh when you can.
It is cheap medicine.
Lord Byron

The wish for healing has always
been half of health.
Seneca

Earth has no sorrow that
Heaven cannot heal.
Thomas Moore

Cats might not take too kindly to commands like "Sit!" or "Stay!" or "Heel!" Yet they're teachable – that is, if they want to be. Showing a kitten how to use a cat door from house-to-screened porch might take a few tries, but if the kitty likes the porch, she's likely to be an attentive student!

Lifelong Learner

As adults, we're fortunate to have so many life-enriching, learning opportunities. No longer is academia or the pursuit of extra-curricular activities just for kids!

The spiritual life, too, is a lifelong learning experience. At no point can we say, "I've learned enough," or "I can stop reading the Bible now." And why would we want to? The more we grow in knowledge and maturity, the more of God's Word we're able to understand and apply to our thinking and behavior. Our constant immersion in spiritual teachings opens us to God's guidance in the challenges we face in our everyday lives.

Let Him open the door to your continuing spiritual education. Learn from Him. No matter how young or old you are, remain teachable.

Dear God, never let me stop learning from You! Keep me always attentive to Your Word.
Amen

Teach me good judgment and knowledge:
for I have believed in thy commandments.
Psalm 119:66

As a single footstep will not make
a path on the earth, so a single thought
will not make a pathway in the mind.
To make a deep physical path, we walk again
and again. To make a deep mental path,
we must think over and over the kind
of thoughts we wish to dominate our lives.
Henry David Thoreau

The one eternal lesson for us all
is how better we can love.
Henry Drummond

I am still learning.
Michelangelo

It matters little where a man
may be at this moment;
the point is whether he is growing.
George MacDonald

One learns by doing the thing;
for though you think you know it,
you have no certainty until you try.
Sophocles

Thy word is a lamp unto my feet,
and a light unto my path.
Psalm 119:105

We must always change, renew,
rejuvenate ourselves;
otherwise we harden.
Johann Wolfgang von Goethe

"A penny for your thoughts, sweet kitty! With your paws tucked in neatly and your tail swooped around you just so, you look to be pondering the mysteries of life. And maybe you are! Perhaps a world, sufficient and complete, lies behind your knowing eyes. Perhaps everything you need lives within your heart."

What's Inside?

God made each one of us with a place inside that is His alone to fill. It's the essence of our true selves, our heart's yearning, that compels us to invite Him in and let His Sprit kindle the flame of our spiritual life.

Yet in our natural longing for God, we often substitute something other than God. It could be anything. Wealth. Fame. Status. Possessions. Relationships. Of course, when we pursue those things thinking they will fulfill us, we're sooner or later proven wrong. Though they are not wrong in themselves, they can't do what God does – provide complete peace and absolute sufficiency. Only after He lives inside can we strive for things outside in a healthy and God-pleasing way. It's what's inside that counts!

Dear God, fill up my heart with longing for You, and not the things that cannot fulfill me.
Amen

All men seek happiness. This is without exception. Whatever different means they employ, they all tend to this end....

A trial so long...should certainly convince us of our inability to reach the good by our own efforts....

What is it then that this craving and this inability proclaim but that there was once in man a true happiness, of which all that now remains is the empty print and trace? This he tries in vain to fill with everything around him, seeking in things absent the help he cannot find in things present? But none can help, because this infinite abyss can be filled only with an infinite and immutable Object; that is to say, only by God Himself.

Iaise Pascal

The great blessings of mankind are within us and
within our reach; but we shut our eyes,
and like people in the dark, we fall foul upon the
very thing we search for, without finding it.
Seneca

What lies behind us and
what lies before us are tiny matters
compared to what lies within us.
Oliver Wendell Holmes

You traverse the world in search of happiness,
which is within the reach of every man.
A contented mind confers it on all.
Horace

The kingdom of God is within you.
Luke 17:21

*Belled and squeaky toys
scattered across the floor.
Bottom shelves bereft of anything breakable. A rumpled
throw that seems to be purring.
Don't blame the housecleaner!
These are the happy signs that a
cat has made this house a home.*

Home Furnishings

What makes your home "home"? For many, it's not possessions themselves, but the memories attached to them. Say a curio cabinet you remember from your childhood days, or the framed photos of loved ones. Or maybe souvenirs from a memorable trip, or gifts you have received over the years from family and friends.

How about the rest – the arrangement of your furniture, the colors of your walls and accessories, the items you see as you walk through your home every day? Do they make you smile with pleasure? Do they comfort you after a tiring day? Do they reflect who you are now? What makes a house a home lies not so much in what is there, but the thoughts and feelings they bring to mind.

Thank You, dear God, for all I have around me that brings me feelings of warmth, comfort, gladness, and gratitude.
Amen

There is no place more delightful
than one's own fireside.
Cicero

Home is a place not only of strong affections,
but of entire unreserved;
it is life's undress rehearsal, its backroom,
its dressing room.
Harriet Beecher Stowe

The ordinary acts we practice every day
at home are of more importance to the soul
than their simplicity might suggest.
Thomas Moore

The power of finding beauty
in the humblest things makes
home happy and life lovely.
Louisa May Alcott

Stay, stay at home,
my heart and rest;
Home-keeping hearts
are the happiest.
Henry Wadsworth Longfellow

Whatsoever things are true,
whatsoever things are honest,
whatsoever things are just,
whatsoever things are pure,
whatsoever things are lovely,
whatsoever things are of good report;
if there be any virtue, and if there be any praise,
think on these things.
Philippians 4:8

Cats aren't noted for their patience. If they want you to open a door, they want it opened now. If they're ready for dinner, they expect a full food bowl set in front of them now. If they're ready to play, their human companion had better be ready, too – now!

God Timing

"Please, God, give me patience, and I want it now!" While the saying brings a smile, it frequently reflects our thinking. When there's something we want to take place, we see no reason for delay.

God's timetable, however, is not the same as ours. Indeed, He knows when we're ready to receive, so He gives at just the right time. He knows when we're prepared to move from one life stage to the next, from where we are now toward where we are going. Maybe today has something to teach so we can fully benefit from the blessings He has in store tomorrow. Maybe now just isn't the time. Yes, pray passionately for what you want! But leave the timing to Him.

**Dear God, grant me the gift
of wholehearted prayer...
and the grace to patiently wait.
Amen**

Meow, Meow, Meow!

Meow, meow, meow! I want it now,
And not a moment later!
The more I wait, I'm more irate,
My wants grow even greater!

Meow, meow, meow! I don't see how
You cannot see my reason!
Now let's get real, why do you feel
This isn't yet the season?

Meow, meow, meow! I want it now,
and it is my fixation —
I'll sit and pout, meow and shout,
Expressing my vexation!

To every thing there is a season,
and a time to every purpose under the heaven.
Ecclesiastes 3:1

Take time for all things:
great haste makes great waste.
Benjamin Franklin

Of all the qualities of an excellent character,
patience is enough for us.
Michel de Montaigne

Not my will, but thine, be done.
Luke 22:42

Patience means waiting without anxiety.
Francis de Sales

Let it first blossom,
then bear fruit, then ripen.
Epictetus

"Well, hello, little one! You, too, have come out to wrap yourself in the scent of lilies, lilacs, and roses. You step gingerly among the tender shoots of newly planted seeds, and you stop to drink from the trickling fountain. And then you rest in the abundance of it all! I, too, put down my trowel and taste the God-blessed stillness."

Natural Wonder

Dedicated gardeners often mention the sense of peace that comes with a cool, quiet morning spent among their plants. Some of our most treasured vacation memories are of glowing sunsets, turquoise seas, or winding wooded paths. To those open to its gifts, nature provides an unending source of serenity, wonder, and beauty.

Even if you are not among those green-thumb growers or happy travelers, you can still open yourself to the tranquility of creation. Notice the color of the sky and the pattern of the clouds. Stop a moment to admire a tree swaying in the distance, savor the scent of spring in the breeze, or delight in a single bloom in a flower shop's bouquet.

Nature is God's gift to everyone. Receive it with joy!

Dear God, open my eyes to the beauty all around me, and let me delight in the work of Your hands!
Amen

The heavens declare the glory of God;
and the firmament sheweth his handiwork.
Psalm 19:1

I never for a day gave up listening
to the songs of our birds,
or watching their peculiar habits,
or delineating them in the best way I could.
John James Audubon

The earth has music for those who listen.
William Shakespeare

In all things of nature,
there is something of the marvelous.
Aristotle

The voice of the sea speaks to the soul.
Kate Chopin

I'll tell you how the Sun rose–
A Ribbon at a time.
Emily Dickinson

There is a blessing in the air,
Which seems a sense of joy to yield
To the bare trees, and mountains bare,
And grass in the green field.
William Wordsworth

Live in the sunshine, swim the sea,
Drink the wild air's salubrity.
Ralph Waldo Emerson

"Well, I haven't seen this before!" That might be exactly what goes through the feline mind whenever he spots something new. A bag of groceries on the kitchen counter, a just-delivered box sitting in the hallway, a storage tub pulled out from the closet – this calls for serious scrutiny! Who knows what interesting item is hiding inside?

What's New?

Most of us have had the experience: Our route is so familiar that we get home and realize we don't remember any of the landmarks we undoubtedly passed! It happens because we're so familiar with the scenery that we're not even seeing it anymore. Yet something could be there that's wonderfully, startlingly new – did we notice?

In the landscape of everyday life, little opportunities frequently peek through the familiar... small gems lying in plain sight that we overlook because we're not expecting them. Say a new face in the crowd pleading for someone to say "hello"...an associate intending to probe our interest in an opportunity, but we nod and keep on walking...a pertinent notice that doesn't catch our eye because we merely glanced in its direction.

What's new? Attentive living will keep you up to date!

Dear God, help me pay attention today!
Help me see what's new in my life!
Amen

A day dawns, quite like other days;
in it, a single hour comes,
quite like other hours;
but in that day and in that hour,
the chance of a lifetime faces us.
Maltbie Babcock

I wish the days to be as centuries, loaded, fragrant.
Ralph Waldo Emerson

Habits are like a cable.
We weave a strand of it every day
and soon it cannot be broken.
Horace Mann

So here hath been dawning
Another blue Day:
Think wilt thou let it
Slip useless away.
Thomas Carlyle

Great opportunities come to all,
but many do not know they have met them.
The only preparation to take advantage of them is
simple fidelity to what each day brings.
Albert Elijah Dunning

Only that day dawns to which we are awake.
Henry David Thoreau

I long to put the experience of fifty years
at once into your young lives, to give you
at once the key to that treasure chamber
every gem of which has cost me tears and
struggles and prayers, but you must work
for these inward treasures yourself.
Harriet Beecher Stowe

God gives the nuts
but he does not crack them.
Proverb

Cats can be finicky eaters.
But what we see as finicky could
be their power of discernment.
In a bowl of food, for example,
their keen sense of smell can
detect a tainted ingredient. As
they approach a small opening,
their whiskers help them judge
whether they can fit through.
A cat's hesitation may be quite
well-founded!

Choose the Good

In our effort not to judge, we often neglect discernment. While judging denounces, discernment is a matter of prudence and perceptiveness. Prudence because we are wise to choose carefully the friends we make and the ideas we support. Perceptiveness because we grow in understanding when we're willing to consider different points of view.

When you evaluate the world around you, look through the lens of God's Word. Is the behavior you witness good, kind, supportive, and God-pleasing? Are the words you hear free of selfish motives? Are they true? Will this person encourage you in your spiritual life? Will these thoughts and ideas inspire personal growth and your ability to influence others for the good?

Practice discernment. Stand up for what you find to be true.

Dear God, help me to choose friends who will grow with me and thoughts that reflect Your will.
Amen

Do not quench the Spirit.
Do not treat prophecies with contempt but test
them all; hold on to what is good.
1 Thessalonians 5:19-21 NIV

As children of the light, we must be careful
to keep ourselves open to every ray of light.
Let us, then, cultivate an attitude of courage
as over against the investigations of the day.
None should be more zealous in them than we.
None should be more quick to discern truth
in every field, more hospitable to receive it,
more loyal to follow it wherever it leads.
B. B. Warfield

Faith is the divine evidence whereby the spiritual
man discerneth God, and the things of God.
John Wesley

The strongest principle of growth
lies in the human choice.
George Eliot

The first point of wisdom is to discern
that which is false; the second,
to know that which is true.
Lactantius

Our greatest power is the power of choice;
our greatest freedom lies in the exercise
of our power of choice.
George William Curtis

Where there is not discernment,
the behavior even of the purest soul may
in effect amount to coarseness.
Henry David Thoreau

Choose the good.
Isaiah 7:15

The power of choosing good and evil
is within the reach of all.
Origen

The whirr of a vacuum cleaner...the roar of thunder...the bark of a dog...the approach of a stranger...any one of these can send a cat into hiding! And she's likely to stay out of sight until the offending machine is put away, the skies have cleared, the dog and the stranger have left her territory. Then it's safe to come out!

It's Only a Vacuum Cleaner!

While some of us are more timid than others, no one is completely free of fear. There's at least one "bump in the night" that finds even the bravest among us trembling!

All your fears, even those you have kept safely hidden from your closest friends, are known by God. He sees inside your heart, not for the purpose of revealing those things you would like to remain private, but to provide you with heart-deep comfort and understanding. There is nothing that happens in the darkest of nights that escapes His all-seeing eye. Put all your fears in His hands. Big bump in the night or only a vacuum cleaner, He is your shelter. He is the One who calms your fears.

Dear God, grant me courage in the face of my fears, and comfort in knowing that You are with me always.
Amen

Fear not, little flock; for it is your
Father's good pleasure to give
you the kingdom.
Luke 12:32

Fear makes the wolf bigger than he is.
Proverb

Do the thing you fear and the
death of fear is certain.
Ralph Waldo Emerson

Nothing in life is to be feared,
it is only to be understood.
Marie Curie

Courage consists not in hazarding
without fear; but being resolutely
minded in a just cause.
Plutarch

One of the effects of fear is to
disturb the senses and cause things
to appear other than what they are.
Miguel de Cervantes

Dare, and the world always yields;
or, if it beats you sometimes,
dare again, and it will succumb.
William Makepeace Thackeray

He shall give his angels charge over thee,
to keep thee in all thy ways.
Psalm 91:11

We must have courage to be happy.
Henri-Frédéric Amiel

She gives me "the look."
She watches me open the can
of choice paté and spoon her
food into her dish. I set it in front
of her. She looks at it, and then
back up at me. "The look"
ranges from "Is that all there
is?" to "You want me to eat
this?" But as soon as I turn my
back, she delves into the dish.
Minutes later, it's licked clean.

The Look

We might not be quite as up-front with our discontent as a finicky feline, yet disappointment can easily take hold in the heart. It's tempting to compare our lives with the lives of others, especially through their posts on social media. Why are they having all the fun?

Of course, posts of birthday parties, family outings, and exotic vacations do not tell the whole story. Each of us faces certain struggles, perhaps even serious challenges. What's most important is not the fun we do (or don't) have, the burden we do (or don't) carry, but how we look at it. When we view all aspects of our life with the eyes of gratitude, contentment fills the heart. And where contentment lives, peace and joy take up residence, too.

Dear God, let my heart rejoice in the good fortune of others, and give thanks for all the blessings in my life.
Amen

No man can be poor that has enough;
nor rich, that covets more than he has.
Seneca

Godliness with contentment is great gain.
1 Timothy 6:6

Don't judge each day by the harvest you reap,
but by the seeds that you plant.
Robert Louis Stevenson

I am always content with what happens,
for I know that what God chooses
is better than what I choose.
Epictetus

When we cannot find contentment in ourselves
it is useless to seek it elsewhere.
François de La Rochefoucauld

The Menu

Finicky kitty, what will it be –
Baked salmon with cheese
Or beef Bolognese?

Finicky kitty, what do you wish –
Fresh cream and flaked fish
To fill up your dish?

Delicate morsels, gravy and meat,
Or savory treat?
Finicky kitty, let's eat!

Someone once remarked that despite the seemingly infinite range of clips available on the internet, cute kitten videos remain the most popular and widely shared! An exaggeration, perhaps, but few cat-lovers are immune to the lure of watching little kitties at play, jostling one another for toys, jumping at feathers, and chasing shadows and sunbeams.

Take a Break

In the middle of a busy day, we're apt to feel guilty taking time out to get some fresh air, chat with a friend, or watch a video of frolicking cats. Yet doing any one of these things pulls the mind away from the day's problems, if for only a few minutes. A short indulgence in "me time" often is all it takes to retrieve our energy, reclaim our thoughts, and restore our sense of balance and purpose.

Tall to-do list? Big problem? Give yourself a break. If you aren't blessed with a kitten or two to play with, a video will do. And the smile on your face is sure to cut lists and problems down to size!

**Dear God, teach me how to
step back and enjoy
the little pleasures around me every day.
Amen**

That man is a success who has lived well,
laughed often, and loved much.
Robert Louis Stevenson

If you are too busy to laugh,
you are too busy.
Proverb

Mirth is God's medicine.
Everybody ought to bathe in it.
Henry Ward Beecher

Laughter is the sensation of
feeling good all over and showing it
principally in one place.
Josh Billings

Seriousness shows itself more majestically
when laughter leads the way.
Heinrich Heine

What comes from the heart,
goes to the heart.

Samuel Taylor Coleridge

Those who bring sunshine to the lives
of others cannot keep it from themselves.

James M. Barrie

Remember, men need laughter
sometimes more than food.

Annie Fellows Johnston

Let us be grateful to the people
who make us happy;
they are the charming gardeners
who make our souls blossom.

Marcel Proust

"It's been a good day, hasn't it, sweet kitty? We've had our adventures...yours, for sure, with a few long naps in between, a day with much more time to sit and watch and dream. So now we'll rest awhile, my book in hand, you nestled in my lap, and we'll savor the peace of an evening hour. Sometimes, it's the quietest moments that speak most deeply of love."

Taste and See

Love is only a feeling unless loving actions follow. When love motivates the things we do and say, we want nothing less than the best we can do for those we care about. We willingly and unselfishly give them our time and attention, not because we have to, but because we want to.

God's great love for you reveals itself in the things He says and does for you. He declares His love repeatedly in the words and promises, guidance and counsel, of Scripture. His actions, too, reflect that love. Through the gifts of His Spirit, He nourishes your heart and mind, enabling you to grow in wisdom and confidence, patience and understanding, joy, peace, and contentment – not because He has to, but because He wants to.

Why wait? Taste and see the love God has for you!

Thank You, dear God, for welcoming me into the blessedness of Your forever love!
Amen

Welcome Home

This is what I have to give,
my little one with golden eyes...
a dish of savory food,
a bowl of fresh, cool water...
a basket of bouncy balls, tinkling bells,
and frisky, fluttery feathers...
a tasty treat, saucer of milk,
a soft, sweet pillow to sleep on...
and loving arms to enfold you
in your forever home.